Incident
at the
Edge
of
Bayonet
Woods

Incident at the Edge of Bayonet Woods

For Jeannette —

With my very best wishes —

poems

Paula Bohince

Paula Bohince

Sarabande S Books
LOUISVILLE, KENTUCKY

FIRST EDITION

Managing Editor
Sarabande Books, Inc.
2234 Dundee Road, Suite 200
Louisville, KY 40205

Library of Congress Cataloging-in-Publication Data

Bohince, Paula, 1976–
Incident at the edge of Bayonet Woods :
poems / by Paula Bohince. — 1st ed.
p.   cm.
ISBN 978-1-932511-62-8 (pbk. : alk. paper)
I. Title.

PS3602.O443I53 2008
811'.6—dc22   2007033692

ISBN-13: 978-1-932511-62-8

Cover and text design by Charles Casey Martin

Manufactured in Canada
This book is printed on acid-free paper.

Sarabande Books is a nonprofit literary organization.

NATIONAL
ENDOWMENT
FOR THE ARTS

This project is supported in part by an award from the
National Endowment for the Arts.

THE KENTUCKY ARTS COUNCIL

The Kentucky Arts Council, a state agency in the Commerce
Cabinet, provides operational support funding for
Sarabande Books with state tax dollars and federal funding
from the National Endowment for the Arts, which believes
that a great nation deserves great art.

Contents

Three

ONE

Prayer

Adore me, Lord,
beneath this raw milk sky, your vision
of silvery cream comprising daylight.

I've kept our appointment
in the barn, board after board of pine
hewn by us,

sit beside the pig we chose
for his mildness
who smiles, now, in his waste.

I abide by the chickadee
who stutters in, a little obsessed
with the mirrored chimes, her baffled image.

Our saddles, oiled on thick nails,
gleam from the walls like 3-D portraits.
Something must be wrong

or else you would answer—
my father in heaven who speaks to me
when no one else will speak to me.

Landscape with Sheep and Deer

I remember the arrhythmia of their movement
across the drenched pasture,
stuttering by my father would say.
What I'm trying to say is remote as a cloud
passing through woods, his face
in a window above the pen,
a clot of feeling.

This must be about him, that man who kept them
jailed and fed, who would not segregate.
In his mind, they were one thing, moving through
one place: sheep of the earth,
the cloud-like sheep, and the earth-toned deer
that belonged to the sky.

Each morning, I filled the feed drum.
Each day, I unlocked the gate, meaning I slipped
a loop from one post to another. The slack
of their limbs meant hunger; their eyes coming toward me
was the anthem I lived by.

O bookish sheep, painterly deer.

Radiant heather and tiny white tongues of clover,
soil glittering with the misery of rain.

I felt something then
in the approximate bones of a field mouse,
horse flies spinning in the trough
alert to the softening presence in the yard.

I fought nothing.
Every morning, I woke up knowing who I was,
that the fence was real, its barbed wire,
those rusted knots, salt lick
glowing like a lamp.

And though I can still see pretty hooves lifting,
feel the purchase of the nozzle
firing fresh water,

I must have dreamt it.

Weren't we always cold?
We wore no wool, had no money from schemes
of shearing and selling the stuff.

And if there were deer, wouldn't they have leapt over?

How can I remember the gentle assemblage
of clucks and hums that drew them
if there were no birth cries, not one buried?

I taste the odor of straw and millet released into fall,
the cursive of my father's burning cigarette,
muslin curtain parting.

Where Radio Fails

In static, four kit foxes turn their alert faces
toward the underbrush where they flicker,
orange as candlelight.

Only their light is insufficient,
smeared by the gauzy ruin of October rain.

Weird cables of the sycamore rattle.

And if the interference of finches on those self-same branches
sends no comfort, no wonder:
those mutants, half-born and flustered,
have no plan for winter.

Meanwhile, the snow geese are flying.
Legs folded, black straps tucked under, they are
winners, bodies clearly superior.

Still, there is a decided purity in the fox heads.

Ears tented; even in wetness
the foxes, slender and seemingly boneless, wash
every inch, each flaming hair
a lit filament.

Trespass

Father's paroled during the drought
of seventy-eight only to vanish again, this time
taking me with him—
stealing into Levi's pasture for cow skeletons,
sun-stripped and patiently gleaming
between the crushed iris.

Above and around us, the electric fence
hums like God—
a magnification of the dreaming gnats we awakened
discovering the lode of bones.

Collecting skull, rib, sternum, spine, the dead
rise, and we forget to be afraid,
thinking only of profit, new lives:

bird earrings from breastbone, the knife-stroke
of feather, fish candlesticks
from femur, long and tapered as sabers.

Escaping through acres where the living cattle
study us, an ache
in language-less throats, we struggle
to carry home all we can hold, glancing heavenward
with knowing, with eyes growing large
all over our bodies.

Black Lamb

Violate, coal-rubbed,

like a word emboldened in an empty book
or a pearl, dark silver, loose
in chamois, pressed into my palm one Christmas...

His thumb upon my thumb, his eyes
on my eyes, and everything is understood: the trespass,
the lamb, the body that will come
to loathe itself,

for even in moonlight, black lamb cannot hide,
cannot fade into the chalky path
as white sheep do.

Black has a singular weight. Painted,
achieves luminous transparency, so that any pistol,
any night sea, shines plainly.

By such proof, my lamb was a phantom. Its kink
and dread reflected nothing.

Profane this landscape, my widening
pupil, drossy with grass charred and spiked short after
a fire; maggots milky in the abattoir's eaves,

black lamb deep in troublesome clover,
alone, quaking beneath dwarf pines.

Hide Out

Stiff as a fish
in a boat, I lie in the grove
of crabapples,
inhaling dirt's pepper, my cheek
wet against stubble,
eye to mineral eye,

tracing the bodies of fish
onto woods' floor—infinity in mud,
curves of hourglass
repeating—

until I cannot hear
my breathing,

until the figure beside the barn,
aerating hay, becomes
a stranger no bigger
than a finger, his pitchfork a flimsy sliver,
harmless rhythm.

When bronze begins to erase
my drawings, pleats the elephant
leaf, when he vanishes,

I grip the girlish cheeks
of crabapple

and pound them and pound them
against ground.

I eat their mush, the grit
pummeled into it,
to coax out the sadness that waits for me
each evening
and cannot be extinguished.

Acrostic: Mementos

Miniatures from a shrunken life, safe,
examined in secret sadness: button with no dress left,
map torn in half, jagged turquoise
ending in his hand, completing the lifeline.
Nothing added for twenty years, each
treasure a snapshot of his child's face, which holds the same
old urges, remnants of that girl. He touches them,
sorry and beyond apologies.

Longlegs

Abdomen small as a mole
on a cheek, as magnetic, but mostly near
nothing—transparent limbs
stilt-walking through the cracked-open window and into
the sunroom where Father,
thin as his mattress, tosses on the bony cot.

Longlegs, drawn by such heat
and sweat, wracked inhales,
exhales, tumbles toward his face,

a frail monster unafraid of the lingering smell
of hand-fed pigeons, the kerosene jug's
glistening mouth.

Soon this will all be over, soon...

Button at my throat, ruffle
at my feet, I look to its shadow long on the sheet,
then to its body,
a kernel, something to be crushed,

woods' chill seeping in
over all I cannot touch: the unlovely man, the whistle
coming through time, the pond
I'd run from, into his arms.

Silhouette

Ankle-deep in freezing mud, clothed by the bristle
of November evening, the kettle blackness
she was born into, my little horse
struggles against the *fallingness*,
as I do,

though today I watched the moons of her hooves
swing between Father's knees
as he pried a month's muck from her iron shoes,
and felt as free as the snuff-colored clumps
that flew, in bumps and skids,
toward the clover.

But now my darling shivers against the horizon,
her henna mane faintly blowing.

This pasture is owned by a ghost
who turns meaner each hour.

Fog breath, sunlight a syrup hung on fence posts,
some unseen dog barking, chipping away
at what tries to gather, what I perceive
as an owl circling above her unprotected body,
trying to lower itself like a saddle,

this owl-horse shape a die the dark impresses
upon our land like a threat
against the living.

Acrostic: Outhouse

Once this homestead held many children,
uncles and great-uncles, delicate and stooping aunts
tatting lace all day, needles replacing
husbands who disappeared into Bayonet Woods, never returning,
obsession becoming gems of fine knots
until their men thread wholly into white roses,
sadly filigreed, as the wild roses
edging the outhouse are eaten by beetles.

Spirits at the Edge of Bayonet Woods

Crabgrass thickens, and catalpas bloom
gigantic, hoping to hide our homestead, the poverty
and grime that kept us mired here
for generations, as if we were sleeping
off a bender for one hundred years.
Sooty hankies against our mouths, in the kitchen
chicken spitting in the fryer,
thick smoke rising, and we're in the mineshafts,
the ones that swallowed our men
and cooked them and spat them into our beds.
Forgive us, Lord, we did not know them,
humpbacked and ruined, crawling toward us
wanting clean shirts, kisses, more children.
Tell me, what was a woman's purpose in those woods?
Trading quails' eggs for the babies' medicine,
boiling ash and animal grease to shampoo coal dust
from our men's curling hair?
They clung to us in sleep, that watery place,
and we swear, as we lay beside our own husbands
we did not know them, even as they struck us,
muttering terrors, whimpering the struggle
of slowly drowning in a shaft flood, or burning
alive in a coke fire. And though we pitied Grace,
the valley's only suicide, we understood
when she wrote, *I cannot go on here, in this place...*
In fact, we watched her strip beside Stone Path
where she had gone to pray, faithful to the current's

constant swirling, watched her weep beside
the river's illiterate banks, lay her dress upon
its slick grasses, wade into the inch of loam,
then lie facedown in its merciful pull.
Forgive her, Lord, for leaving this earth so early.
She was terribly lonely.

Johnstown

When a girl is raped, left crumpled in a tree stand
wearing only a muzzle of ice, her mermaid hair frozen
in weird angles, my father and I start talking.

Say how, after the great flood, the drowned were found
as far west as the Ohio—in trees, in chimneys—
so the governor ordered all water between be dragged,
putting to bed a dozen cold cases.

We read aloud, relearn how experts knew it was coming,
draw pictures of bodies caught in a sprawl.

We cut her out, mail the grain of her eyelids, wet ink
of her hair, to relatives who've left. Here in Johnstown,
we drift between the missing and the dead.

Quarry

Supposed dragnet for the past, but that net is empty
save for a few scattershot leaves, a limp posy blown wide open.

Better if I could lie eye-level with this ocean,
if I could quarrel with these rocks, woo outrage the way
I woo sorrow.

There ought to be a slow-forming fire somewhere,
not these pale mists, which are moths, which are offerings of light
to the foiled landscape.

If I could raise my eyes to the house, its frost-stained window,
where my father sits beside his shaving mug
and brush, his face looking out onto the rest of his life...

Greenish stubble of weeds waiting for some emotion to occupy it,
though emptiness is its own kind of balm.

Oriole

Consider three orioles—
black and orange in virgin snow,
definite against vapor—

as a single oriole
with a triune nature:

one on the fence, divider
of gifts, another who is pure
ornament, posed stoically
on the fir,

and a third who is wise,
the oracle
playing against his fate—
dashing from feeder to feeder,
pummeling the seed bell.

I love these firebirds
for their toughness, for resisting
my usual lens of pity,

who frighten me
as the football players used to
years ago, in church—

their bruised bodies
suited onto an opposite field,
who stood among us,
alarmingly still.

Brutally, the Robin

clutches the clear muscles of the ice-
laden branches.
Without a scrap, without a word
he is sentenced
in red pajamas like a deposed king. This is the world's
revenge against masculine beauty: the bold color
it granted it withdraws, whole, in bold statement.
His eyes are black-rimmed, his fluted bones
could lift if they wanted.
But where, at this late hour? To what embassy?
He belongs to the void now, that prairie,
and is starving, I said.

Two

The Apostles

Begin with a paper bag
flush with crumpled hundreds, begin
with the body of it,
hidden in a trick drawer or mattress,
then count up to ten thousand,
the bills like garbage, but for a green
like the eyes

of a man who thought banks
meant foreclosure, debt, this man
arrested months before my birth
for petty theft, jailed three years, reborn
as a farmer, who paid his laborers
from this sack.

Then think of those men
who drove up each morning, caps low
over their faces, who may have felt
cheated, ruined, furious
at this man who barely had anything—
an inherited homestead, a few
aging animals...

And if they surprised him
one Saturday night, he would have seen
friends—John, Lucas, Paul—
my apostles, he'd joke, bringing loose talk

and whiskey, and if they wanted to see
the money, if they spun a gun
and wanted money,

and if they finished him
with one shot through the ribs, left him
to bleed beside his bed,
there is no evidence.

Spent now, what was left of a life—
divided three ways, blown all over town.

The Gospel According to Lucas

The day's meanest pleasure:
threading worm after worm, entire
length and breadth,
onto our hooks—
souls hardened, visible at last
beneath translucent flesh.

This, and the praise my boss offers
as payment, calling me *son,*
goddamning my gifts,

while the fish, experts
in the discipline of water, the element
we borrow, fell for our tricks,
landing pathetic,
heavy in the basket between us:

the bluegill we should have sent back,
easy between our hands,
bluegill we will not eat
or admire.

Our lines cast out softly
from the furred edge of sedge, algae,
my intent to be a good man
filled with mercy

erasing as evening overwhelms,
as the argument within myself increases
in sense and volume.

The Fish of Galilee

Many derived from the one, wonder replicated publicly
into proof. Look now upon the aqua bodies, the wooden table.
A fish is lifted, twitching, and also there is bread
famous for its seeds, empty bramble baskets. There is salt
in His beard, saline of belief curling it, there are faces
waiting to be fed. Transported from the sea, silver-eyed,
they are handed to knived women. The slaughter of thousands
is ordinary, robotic. Currency trembles slightly in grease,
the meal is uneasy. Perfume of blood and pickling, the plates
lie pearly, blank: they have that quality.

Eating Fish in Pittsburgh

Tense in the booth, I wait
by leaning in,
fingers knotted in a double-prayer.

Wearing my father's red sweater,
his face, I am burning
his death

over emptied baskets of waxed paper,
windows of grease,
the memory of cod.

Newly wedded, bound
to grief, our home
the single room of a car,

I drive and I cry, same routine:
my head against the glass,
mouth in a heaving square

sometimes speaking, *I don't want
to die, but I can't help it—
I can't get this feeling out.*

And I would take my body
into the clatter of a dive,
and they saw me as a kid,

normal, gave me fish, tore my page
from their book.
I could count on that

and the rain,
the smell of fish oil in my clothes,
the bones I kept, as gifts.

The Fatherless Room

Electric as wasps unfurled from a dresser,

literal wasps that were sleeping
in drawers lined with torn bills and sugar packets
like unopened envelopes.

A humidifier haloed in watermarks.

Meanwhile, the white-wigged branches and wrens
go on like nothing's missing.

They make a cocoon for the mind.

When the eye is bruised from looking
at worms dried in half-circles
and carpet starry with blood and gunpowder,

there is the shorn field and snow
to make a lacy curtain.

Because truly the carpet is blood-wrecked.
And the floorboards beneath it.

If this were spring, there would be more birds
to look at. *My* birds, I would think,
in these trees that were his.

Cleaning My Father's House

I've come home, to sit inside this house
among the locusts and the crickets, their goodbye duet,
their chitter and squeak of *So long*.
Packing his things to make room for my own:
his pale blue Easter suit, his Bowie knife, its leather sheath
branded with *Nashville*. Catholic medals,
a finger's length statue of Christ in agony on the cross.
I touch the open mouth and put Him away.
So much stuff engraved upon a life. His wallet,
like a miniature and battered suitcase, still feels warm.
How can that be? Social security card
soft as dishcloth, his license, expired now, a laminated
girlie picture behind it—blond barrel curls,
angora sweater unbuttoned.
I find the flannel shirts I gave him one Christmas,
press them to my lips, hungry for his scent of gasoline
and tobacco, pomade and Ivory soap.
Beneath the bed, slippery piles of Stagger Lee and Lena
Horne records, a dozen half-carved
wooden animals. Biographies of Custer, Billy the Kid.
I think my father was a boy, an unhappy child
who played with guns and trouble, who had a daughter
by accident, each of us bewildered by the other.
It's dark outside, end of the longest summer.
We met once, in this life. Even the ash in his ashtray
seems precious, impossible to be rid of.

Acrostic: Geese in Snow

Gray loses its middling strength, turns purer,
empyreal, blank as the long sleep
eventide courts into its massive bed, bony finger beckoning.
Snow comes, lathering such belled and heavy bodies
erotic in their stillness.
Ice cripples the pond they drink from, the stream—
negatives of what heaven was promised to be.
So where are we?
Noiselessly losing, the geese huddle and must decide, while
overhead there is nothing to help them break,
with wing-beats, this curse.

First Day of the Hunt

The schools always close, knowing
we're so country
all our boys will skip anyway,

and the valley rises together before dawn—

daughters pulling wool caps
past fathers' ears, reciting the profound
and elemental list:

rifle, rounds, knife, rope,

only to send each heavy man to the woods
where he'll slump the day in drifts
of solitude and prayer

while most deer stay down, evading
the unlucky, the night spent

visiting cousins: stroking curves
of antler, lengths of blood-stiffened fur.

Every year it's the same
soft and deliberate snow prints,
the waiting—

as if mine could emerge from his last hiding
place and walk the evening,
empty-handed, to me.

The Gospel According to Paul

A garter snake hushes the grass,
its head like a shovel, its skin the grip of a gun.

I am reminded of what I have done.

She whispers her petty life into my hands:
my work to deliver her from harm.

My sister, dying of cancer, soothed by a hiss
of oxygen, a drip of morphine in blood

slow as the last remnants of rain hanging long
off the sycamore,

then soaring toward earth.

The ravenous mouths of beetles
riddling those same leaves into punched tin,

which I find so beautiful.
Theirs is an innocent hunger.

All my life I have plotted, a snake in the grass,
which I see now as innocent.

Innocent.

Acrostic for My Father

I can't bear the pitiful beauty of our only oak
declining in these ill-lit woods, masculine branches bearing
robins, savage in their redness.
Everything becomes a version of you,
assumes a fern or bird shape, some feathery thing I put want into.
My days are colored by your absence, or left blank,
open-ended. I fill my eyes with reminders.
Fronds I refuse to weed line the house, this lonely house
you left me. The rest of my life you have left me.
Oak leaves fill with crumbling light. So I,
undone by the quiet.

Photographing the Moths

Eruption at the flash: shattered light
swarming the screen door. Whitetail musk behind me,
scent of rhubarb spiked through. Ripped
wings like rag curlers the aunties wore
in girlish sleep, inheriting the hard, day-lit hours.
On the pillow, against the lens, questions of attraction,
Why moths? Why midnight? are lifted. No one home
to ask. No friction of love against reason.

When I Think of Love

I see John in his flowered shirt
chiseling shingles off the roof over my bedroom,
him rainbowed there, in oil and tar,

the rainbow, the memory
dwindling to one sexual minute caught in the sunlit
hollow of his throat, pool deepening

to soil's color by August,
my earth, I imagine, as he turns the fields in autumn,
my sunlight memorizing his body

aloft on the tractor, an image I think I'll die from,
as corn stalks snap beneath tires,
his last name, his address, lost

there in that remote acre of lust where I've hid him
all these years, so that he lives on,
forever nineteen, drinking the cold tea I bring

to this boy who left school at fourteen,
who comes each summer wanting work, then stays,
wanting my life, I believe.

The Gospel According to John

Truth is, God was not present.

Missing when I fell from the tractor,
the cast and sling I wore, my right arm ruined
thereafter.

Truth is, no song
played though chimes in the barn, no voice
pretty in wind.

There was no commandment, no voice
demanding cash but my own.

But what work to live as a son,
what thistle and burr suffered for years.

When the wet rose bloomed
in the chest of the man I killed, I tried to concentrate
on its image,

tried to sit with that flower and feel
as God must:

the pleasure of His birds swollen with feathers,
His birds bound to His sky,

belonging to His kingdom of violence.

Clinging

The dirty sheep cried all night for her mate. In her stall,
a comprehensible world of straw, mushrooms bluish in manure,
long hoof prints of her husband yesterday shuttled away
with three others. This, and the stubborn feathers of the grouse—
lilac, blue-black where it was hit. I'm here too, stripping
the bird of her magic: upside-down, she swings by the feet,
crease of blood on her neck, locket of heart rapt inside her breast.
Over still-wet fields, the lucky ones hobble toward the illusion
of safety that woods allow, while the quills of the dead one
seem to dig in deeper, as if clinging saves anyone.

THREE

Still Life with Needle

Mending by oven heat—
push-pin painted to mimic a peach, its felt
leaf dusty as the black ribbon
I used to snake through my braid
each morning.

And there, wedged in the kit: an orphan
earring, opal pried out,

a mussel shell, smoke-blue, its sand loose
on the satin.

Nightgown limp on my lap, torn
at the shoulder where I leaned hard against
a sycamore, waiting for a comet,
then falling asleep,

feeling myself carried to bed, waking
with dirt in my mouth,
then remembering.

What comfort, these stitches like footprints
unspoiled by a body. Such pure
walking muffles the mind,

and the spray of bridal birds
swerving past the curtain wakes it. *There goes
my wedding,* I'd say as a girl. As every
girl did in the valley.

Toward Happiness

I loved one person all my life.

He who let me hold the saw while he hammered, let me
hold the hammer while he sawed,
his fingers like spigots,

who stormed off, jaw tight with disgust
at my incompetence,

lurching into shade-drawn rooms, knocking over
the sawhorse on his way, clouds
of sawdust for me to sweep,

snoring in a black mood beside the television's
soothing voice, awakening
an amnesiac, asking if the shutters were cut
and sanded, feeling my hands to see
if I was lying.

On the Today Show, a man in a straw hat serenades
his saw, its bend and whine, accompanies
the melody to *Oh Suzanna.*

I'd like to make a noise like that: carefree, optimistic.
Instead, I find the birdhouse pattern in the cellar
between jars of pennies, haystacks

of bent nails: seven squares,
a little hole for a door,

dig out the jigsaw, gather wood scraps while whistling,
not thinking, *This is happiness*.

Idle Hours

Chores over, I duck from the henhouse
into twilight after cleaning eggs our rooster
destroyed in a fury. Him
agitated in a corner, beak slimy
with the unborn. I've broken them
into the skillet before: those curled and featherless
nothings; touched the fused eyelids,
gelatinous legs. I clean my hands in the pond.
The day's dregs wash away...
The racket when I trashed those eggs
I should have tried harder to save, for the hens'
sake, salvaging what I could.
I can't tell what's good or awful anymore,
only what kills the idle hours:
engine in the water seeping oil, minnows
sparking beneath that polished ceiling, weathervane
on the chimney caught in reflection: copper
fisherman casting into heaven.

Farm Triptych

Swimming

That was his gift.
How he swam the swampy length
to impress me, his face
a blurry moon-behind-clouds moon rising
to where I waited
on the warm, slippery banks,
at our pond's soapy edge,
long grasses folded beneath legs, beach towel
in my hands, twisting,
as he sank like a chain to the bottom's
soft decay, roiling for an eternity before
roughing the grave surface
with splashes and hollers.
His cruel nature, the lie of his beauty
beginning there, in that element.

Splitting

Ill, I split logs—
wedge of axe blade wavering
over my head, lost for an instant before
carrying its own weight
down, into the wood's pale niche,

twin bobbins spun off the chopping stump.
This is my life,
bent over splinters, six cords' worth
stacked against the shed's eastern wall.
This is my coat, shaking off cold.
Royal jelly at my nostrils, I eat my thimble
of honey, drink my capful of whiskey,
snow blurring the outhouse
into something pretty.

Sleeping

Thus, he's alive again,
though ashen as the snowball blossoms,
clusters once cut loose, scattered
for my punishment.
He watches me turn beneath the fleur-de-lys
quilt his mother made, certain
of a daughter.
Then I'm with him, in the barn
damp with birdsong, thrushes thrilling the eaves,
air perfected by oat-dust, the sweetness
of kerosene, the breathing of horses
lost to the mortgage.
The dream seduces them
to a life that is gone: the two of us
cooing and caressing those muscular necks,
talking our baby talk.

Pond

Don't be mean to me.
Don't make me look at the swamp
of his body, come spring,
when the job of my childhood was staring:
jaw unhinged, mind agog
at the whitewash of trillium—
whorl of three leaves with a solitary rising flower,
world sickening on the vine,
buds, hoary with sugar, swaying
like appraising hands.

When we're alone, my neighbor Marie
puts her face inside her own hands
moaning, *If I let myself feel...*

She's not dumb. She can tell
she's been touched, if not the *how*,
not the *when*, though she senses the riddle
lies with her father—
pond matting his beard, and her with no rope
or raft to cling to—

the opaque memory making her choose
herself over him.

How can she stay
when the idea of a pond on her property

is terrifying? Spending weeks reading her theories
on why some men fear
and hate women.

Yet here we are: women,
even married, now twice married to the land
of our childhoods,

both with those awful sinkholes
our husbands and fathers love and loved
to look out on,
tempting us to leave this place
where nothing lives,

though even as I claim this, a truckload of kids
has plowed into the banks,
scattering beer cans.
It's their routine; it's their job
as mine is to cross out of myself every day
and enter the world,

an act entirely separate from waking,
separate from picking up cans or finding the key
to my father's old room,
that other wound,
needing to stand where his body lay
for three days before its discovery, in heat,

a desire that is separate, I think,
from wanting him back.

That feeling I check for daily
in the pond, Marie, the dream, this farm.

White Trumpets

In March snow slicing off Bobcat Mountain
Marie unpins Tim's shirts from the line,
recounts her latest vision:
a cougar yesterday, watching her aerate hay.

And so she kept the pitchfork's rhythm perfect.
And so it let her live.

In hand-me-down beds, we wake
to the bittersweet perfume of pine and licorice
the cold can't hide,

pour water, open drawers and stare hard
at tabs of acid, listen to woods
crack and exhale,

glance toward the mountain
where our husbands have made a six-day camp,
navigating the tangle and gulch,
tracking one last illegal shot of bobcat.

Call it anything you want—
cougar, bobcat, husband, hunt, abandonment.

Or else say, *our fields are alight with daffodils,*
those white trumpets we nearly drowned in as children.

Drive-In: The Wizard of Oz

Is this Eden?

Lying in poppy fields, under sleep's spell,
waking to snow's remedy, unharmed, among friends,
nearly at the Emerald City, its Technicolor
horses, Lion's new curls,

green of crushed Rolling Rock glittering,
screen sputtering white while someone changes the reel . . .

Rabbit foot swinging in ignition,
neighboring trucks gunning their engines, beds
flush with firewood, Union numbers
peeling off bumpers, rifles
in rear windows.

In the end, it's the reappearance of those men—
Hunk and Hickory and Zeke—
that scares me. Those farmhands disguised in sepia,
in ordinary clothes, denying her story.

She is hurt in the head, outnumbered.
She changes her mind. To live in the world means
forgetting that dream:

its yellow contagion,
babies waking in nests, poisonous sand in its hourglass,

Scarecrow on fire, her Witches East and West,
those accidents.

Watching Lightning Strike the Walnut

means agreeing the day divides
into *before* and *after*,

and spend its remains wandering the yard
collecting burnt branches,

each reminiscent
of the bough cut down

last year, in April,
after holding death beneath snow's spell,

its denials.
In the ghost, I see my life

shimmering gold all over,
the life of before

I was split down my length and broken.
Know the feeling?

Tree smoking, fire trucks wailing to, body
on the porch, electrified by loss.

Adoration of the Easter Lamb

New to the world, our farm,
is this darling—

gilded with placenta, gluey curls
skull-tight, named
Shelley for its breathlessness, the hazel eyes
that blithely surmise the earth.

Little solemn forehead,
flourish.

Sore body licked raw, cut loose
from love's bonds, from the ordinary
ewe who is terrified
of loving what is doomed.

Put away the nipple's fleshy nub.
Let the formula on the stove boil away.

A painting of a lamb on a dark altar—
bound, asleep-looking:
that's what you are.

Puny creature, beginning to tremble
although it is April and warm.

Come, come.

Resurrection

As evening comes, Mary Magdalene and Mary the mother
inhabit the rubble outside the tomb. A tangle of crying. Ordinary
mourning. Nothing yet risen, no visible alchemy. Only
linen and dust bits hesitating behind stone. Brittle
carapaces of beetles to keep company the human husk. The drama
of earth nearly finished: Judas hanged, silver buried in the fields
of blood. Trio of spirit days in which the women wait, their harmonic
wailing ended. Rustle of the exhausted vessel. Plum pits
roll from fingertips onto ground, flies gathering at the echo
of sweetness. Then He walks out. Brief the reunion. And long
the second grief, with nowhere to keep vigil.

The Fly

Did I invite him with thoughts of sugar?
All day he chased me, trailing
blue dashes, settling in the hot tent of my ear
as a nomad and medium
whose psychic abilities outmatched my own
so I assumed, all afternoon, his mind—
the absolute pleasures of warm flesh,
of washing, balanced on the rippling drum...
There was no room for remembering
a youth that seemed to fall away in minutes,
no space for regret, only a pledge to live
intensely, hovering inches above the body.

Heaven

The heifer grazing by her lonesome
has gold in her mouth, and the mark of lightning
on her forehead.

Who doesn't believe in heaven?

Quicksilver thrushes form a chain
in the stable's eaves; the mosquito drags
her spindly legs across the trough,
shivering as lichen catches,
her engine purring in perfect voice.

Even my little pink house, sliding off the hill,
wants to be caught.

Charity

The .22 hidden from auction
abandons its nine kinds of blackness:
its *choke* and *muzzle*, the *comb*
where his cheek rested, the *heel* digging into his rib
for steadiness, the *rib*
where his sight fit, his *sight*
and *barrel, hammer*
and *trigger*—
mine now.

And the jumpsuit
bereft of a body,
slumped in the hunting closet,
I zip on, even if it means
entering woods' mottled camouflage, leaf after leaf
collaged into a dirty vision, mud-caked fleece
against my skin,
a kind of reverse-heaven.

I wear it for Marie
whose father called her *Golden Dream*
and fed her Quaaludes,
leaving her babbling on the woods' blank stage,
jeans twisted in trees
too high to reach,
fingers splitting the light between branches,

scrapes on her face, floss of sap
in her hair.

That was heaven:
all those years spent talking
across the fence
to a woman whose friendship was like being
alone, in conversation, when we said,
yes, pain and *yes, grief,*

but also *grace*
the body gives itself after great trauma,
as when her father died
from drink, and mine from men
who lived, unfound,
among us.

In church, we sang and read
about God, who has given us such bounty—
this earth, for instance—such given
charity.

But what the Book
omits, what the song, is how He allotted
for each gift one brutality
for balance.

Now, without birds
or the magic of birds, without deer
or the empathy of deer,

those luxuries conjured for my eye,
I try to be honest.

I am done with their images.

What I remember
is one sheep
who left her lamb in summer
to swim in the pond-turned-mud,

her legs filthy, curls
matted and ugly,

gnats strumming softly
It's over, It's over over lily pads that broke
the surface, my hands
holding the rope's crimped end
for hours.

And when I cry, I can hear her still
crying in the loam, stranded,
dazzled by white flowers.

Acknowledgments

Grateful acknowledgment is given to the editors of the publications in which these poems first appeared: *32 Poems*: "The Fatherless Room"; *Agni*: "Adoration of the Easter Lamb," "The Fly"; *The American Poetry Journal*: "Prayer," "Where Radio Fails"; *The Antioch Review*: "Acrostic: Mementos"; *Beloit Poetry Journal*: "Acrostic: Outhouse"; *Cimarron Review*: "Clinging"; *Crazyhorse*: "Black Lamb," "Brutally, the Robin," "Longlegs"; *FIELD*: "Toward Happiness"; *Green Mountains Review*: "Acrostic for My Father," "Quarry"; *International Poetry Review*: "Watching Lightning Strike the Walnut"; *Mississippi Review*: "Johnstown"; *The Nation*: "Hide Out"; *The National Poetry Review*: "Oriole"; *The New Hampshire Review*: "The Fish of Galilee"; *New Orleans Review*: "Landscape with Sheep and Deer"; *Ploughshares*: "Cleaning My Father's House"; *Poetry Northwest*: "Charity"; *Post Road*: "The Gospel According to John," "The Gospel According to Lucas"; *Prairie Schooner*: "Heaven"; *Salmagundi*: "Still Life with Needle"; *Shenandoah*: "Spirits at the Edge of Bayonet Woods"; *Slate*: "First Day of the Hunt"; *Southwest Review*: "Resurrection"; *Spoon River Poetry Review*: "Pond"; *Willow Springs*: "Eating Fish in Pittsburgh"; *The Yale Review*: "Photographing the Moths"

"Silhouette," "Trespass," and "White Trumpets" won the Grolier Poetry Prize for 2005 and appeared in the *Grolier Poetry Prize Annual*.

"The Fly" was reprinted in *Best New Poets 2005* (Samovar Press).

69

"Acrostic: Outhouse" appeared on *Poetry Daily* on March 23, 2006 and was reprinted in *Poetry Daily Essentials 2007* (Sourcebooks).

"Black Lamb," "Brutally, the Robin," "Oriole," "Prayer," "Spirits at the Edge of Bayonet Woods," and "Trespass" reappeared on *From the Fishouse* (www.fishousepoems.org).

Sincere appreciation is given to the MacDowell Colony, the Ludwig Vogelstein Foundation, the Puffin Foundation, and Mary Rosenberg. For their teaching, I thank Lynn Emanuel, Galway Kinnell, Philip Levine, Sharon Olds, and Marie Ponsot. Additional thanks go to Kazim Ali, Frannie Lindsay, and Sara Wallace. I am deeply grateful to Sarah Gorham and Jeffrey Skinner for their guidance and support. For their love, I thank my mother and sister. And I thank my husband Patrick Mullen, for everything.

Patrick Mullen

Paula Bohince grew up in rural Pennsylvania. Her poems have appeared in such publications as *Agni, Michigan Quarterly Review, Ploughshares, Shenandoah, Slate, Southwest Review,* and *The Yale Review*. She has received a "Discovery"/*The Nation* Award, the Grolier Poetry Prize, residencies from the MacDowell Colony, and the Amy Clampitt Resident Fellowship. She has taught at New York University, the New School, and elsewhere, and was the University of Mississippi's inaugural Summer Poet-in-Residence. She holds an MFA from New York University and lives in Pennsylvania.